T0196972

Speak Only Kindnesses

Speak Only *Kindnesses*

Volume 1: Steps to Manifesting Joy in the New Energy

TONI PAGE

BALBOA
PRESS

A DIVISION OF HAY HOUSE

Balboa Press books may be ordered through booksellers or by contacting:

Balboa Press
A Division of Hay House
1663 Liberty Drive
Bloomington, IN 47403
www.balboapress.com
1 (877) 407-4847

Print information available on the last page.

ISBN: 978-1-5043-7227-5 (sc)
ISBN: 978-1-5043-7228-2 (hc)
ISBN: 978-1-5043-7237-4 (e)

Library of Congress Control Number: 2016921284

Balboa Press rev. date: 02/21/2017

This book is dedicated to the many magnificent and loving people in my life. I am thankful, in particular, to all those who expressed their love by taking care of me during and after my two surgeries. They were instrumental in my transformation. My sister, my sons and my dearest friends are truly the models for love in my life.

PREFACE

Speak Only Kindnesses

My story is a simple story. I was changed. Changed by a set of events that, despite my resistance, was to benefit me beyond belief. I do not pretend to understand the mechanics, the who, how or why. I hope this book also changes you.

I was raised Catholic. I gave it up for Lent one year, in 6th grade. I never returned to the organized religion but continued to seek a spiritual connection through an insatiable predilection for reading material that was on the fringe of both spirituality and metaphysics.

My story is about the heart. I had experienced so much heartbreak over such a long period of time, that my heart closed. Yes, I went through the motions: I loved briefly and intensely, and repeatedly, but the unconditional love that originates in the heart was not to be found.

My father died of a heart valve that closed. I was 11. With my first pregnancy, I learned that I, too, inherited a congenitally defective aortic valve … and my valve was closing and would need to be replaced. I managed to delay the open heart surgery until I was 55 by judicious diet, exercise and heart-healthy supplements. I underwent the gruesome surgery in 2010. I became conscious midway through the operation but could not speak or move. Traumatized, I gave up and succumbed to the last sleep. Unexpectedly, however, I woke in pain, groggy, disgruntled and ornery. I had lost my right lung function, had a poorly functioning heart, and could neither walk nor talk normally for months. My esophagus randomly went into noisy spasm. The broken wired-together breastbone hurt relentlessly, and I could not sit up for months without muscle spasms in my back and neck delivering excruciating pain. I remember, as clearly as I remember yesterday, waking alone in the middle of each night, sweating, in pain, and disoriented, with a disgusting medicinal taste in my mouth. It was nearly 9 months before I was able to breathe, walk, talk and return to my work. I vowed I would never undergo such a surgery again. When this valve exhausted its lifetime, I exhausted mine. It was certain.

I did not have an easy time during the years following my surgery. In fact, I was not "nice". I became depressed, fell into bankruptcy, lost resources I had saved over a lifetime, lost my partner to an early death, and came close to losing my job, a career for which I had spent eons in training. I began sleeping 15 -18 hours most days and this went on for about 7 months, jeopardizing my health, social connections and career. I did little else.

Then, the news. The aortic heart valve implanted 5 years before was a bad model. It was failing. I had two months to live. Or, I could agree to the unthinkable - having another surgery, a "re-do". Anesthesia, analgesics, tearing out the old wires and re-breaking the sternum, cutting out the old scar tissue and extricating the bad valve. Stitching in a new one. Pain, disorientation, bedrest, dozens of medications and blood draws, loss of appetite. High risk, uncertain outcome, possibility of permanent life changes.

There was little time for deliberation. I sought guidance from friends, relatives, neighbors, physicians, my sons. I sought guidance from psychic readers, spiritual advisors, the pendulum, kinesiology. I prayed to God, spiritual Guides, and Angels. I turned within. I prepared to go into surgery not caring whether I lived or died. It didn't really matter that much.

And then I had the visions. I can't say when they began. They were with me before during, and after surgery. The image was clear and familiar from my childhood. It was Christ in front of me, slightly to my right, in his soft white robes with his gentle eyes and long brown hair. He was holding out in front of him a new heart … one that was radiating a brilliant white light, and a warmth that was connecting us. I would continue life in this body, provided I chose to share His teachings. I would be gifted with a new heart, and the energy of youth, if I agreed to speak only kindnesses from that day forward. Was this an agreement, a commitment, a contract? I had a new purpose. His message is to bring others to awareness that there is Divinity within each of us, and we are more powerful than we realize.

I woke from surgery in only mild discomfort and was ecstatic! I was joking and laughing with my sister and son as soon as the breathing tube was removed! I joyfully told the cardiac surgeon how great I felt! I was breathing fine within hours. My pulse and blood pressure stabilized. My heart rhythm was entrained by cardioversion. I was surrounded by people that I loved and who loved me. I felt my Spiritual team around me every minute of the days that followed. The love energy was palpable. A dear friend saw "legions of Angels" surrounding me. I experienced a miraculous recovery as I continued to have the vision of Christ offering me the glowing heart each night after surgery, even after I returned home. Within days, I was walking, eating, unmedicated, happy, alert, talking with my loving friends and family of caregivers. I was very conscious and appreciative of my new open, radiating heart. I felt love for whomever fell into my view. I was moved to tears by compassionate actions of those around me, of people in the news. I wept while watching movies. I felt my heart open to friends and strangers alike. I felt more in the days after surgery than in the decades before.

At seven weeks I drove myself to Chicago. At 8 weeks post-surgery I was doing what it took 8 months to manage after the first aortic valve replacement. I felt energetic, strong, healthy and ecstatic to be in my physical body. I have learned how to re-image myself and rejuvenate. Each day I am more connected to and appreciative of all those around me, both physical and non-physical Beings.

I am not the same person I was. I am more loving. I am at peace. I am kinder, patient and accepting. I am more joyful, confident and secure. I have a knowing of my purpose. I gratefully relinquish my previous scientific career for one that involves teaching, comforting and healing others. I have changed and I believe that change is attributable to my encounters with the Christ, the Master, the Teacher. My new heart represents the Christ within. And the Christ energy is within each of us. We need only remember to ask that he speak with us.

I believe that the words in this book are His.

Toni Page

As I sit quietly, first thing in the morning, I receive one-word-at-a-time messages that I write down in my journal. I 'hear' these messages whenever I invite Christ to tell me what I need to know; to teach me what he would have me teach. I have been writing now, most mornings, for over a year. Each time I read the messages I am struck by how new the words feel, like I have never heard them before. I am also amazed that the messages are coherent, loving, and, for me, inspiring. In the spirit of weaving together a kinder, more tolerant world, I share these messages with you.

Listen with an open heart and an open mind.

1

I Am Here

I am here. Do not doubt my presence with or in all of you. All is well. All is goodness.

2

You are Loved Beyond Measure

Do not fear for all is as it should be. Be open in heart and mind and all that is truth will flow through you: So much more than mankind could know without the energy of the Masters. As I said, all energies are one. Yet they flow in different directions much like the rivers that connect with the oceans. All water is one.

Bring love and hope to all those who cry out for a better way. Yes, dear ones, this is similar to a Course on Miracles (COM) in that all who ask now will be met with the better way. All will eventually ask in their own time. Seek peace, let your heart radiate love. Practice the vibration indiscriminately but discern carefully whom you tell for now. No 'convincing' is needed as all are gifted with discernment and the innate knowledge of what is truth. Giving the space to those who need permission is part of the mission. You will touch many lives in ways you cannot know on this Earth. You will have great assistance from many sources and you will succeed in sharing My message and that of Creative Source. Be blessed. You are loved beyond measure. Share it.

At Your Door

3

You Are the Light

No more anger. Love overpowers anger, resentment. You, Dear Ones, have been practicing the feeling of love and appreciation. This has made the transition from your old state to this new energy more gradual and easier for you. Imagine Dear Ones, if all humanity were thrust from survival mode into the love light of Source abruptly! What disorientation would occur! What confusion! How busy would therapists be? If all forgiveness and love funneled through at once, the world you know would grind to a halt - no more competition, lawyers or legal cases, banking would stall, people would not mis-serve others! This change must occur gradually and in perfect timing with the new energies that are being transmitted to and assimilated by your planet. Those who recognize and appreciate the difference in the energy will be the first to latch onto the new and glorious way of life on Earth. Yes, some "old souls" of Earth are among this group and some not. All souls are old souls in that the soul material has been around eternally and will continue to express as more and greater. The soul material morphs continually as every atom in the Universe is continually changing in response to every thought, action, intent and deed everywhere. The message is to continue to pay attention to your thoughts and their vibration. Hold higher vibrations for longer and grow to offer the Universe the greatest gift that you can: Ongoing and conscious love and appreciation of all that surrounds you, presents to you and obstructs you. For in your ever-improving vibration you will more frequently choose the emotion, the power and the love - deliberate love that will change and improve the quality of human life and vibrational harmonies of our Universe. Yes, Dear Ones, it is deliberate and conscious choice that make the difference. You are the light. You are the way. You are loved beyond measure. Share it.

4

Make Peace

Go make your peace with the world, for the world cannot wait.
I can.

5

Resist with Love

There are sharks in the water, Dear Ones. This is metaphor meaning that the dark will attempt to lure you in. It will attempt to regain power. Power over your thoughts, your life, your sense of who you are. Resist. Resist simply. Resist with thoughts and words of joy and love. For where there is the light, the love, the joy, the compassion, there is no room for dark. It lets go it's hold. It flees to approach easier subjects. Eager subjects - and there are sharks in the water. Do not bring lure or bait. Stay on the surface. Allow no one or nothing to force you to acknowledge them. No fear! They cannot sense you. All is dependent on your choices. You are loved beyond measure, Child, Share the love freely, openly and abundantly. So it is.

Leave it Behind

6

Stunning Impact

Let go of your perceptions for they are inaccurate and misleading. Yes, it is true you experience the reality that you create. However, your experience of reality is determined by so much more than merely thought. For the Creative essence has structured a system far beyond your capacity to understand. How this meshes together with your free choices continually changes the vibration of the planet and the Universe. Many probabilities are close to firm in your dimension but play out very differently in others. It is your ability to choose who and what you are that defines you. There is no good, no evil, just a balance of dark and light energies, much like a changing yin-yang symbol. For in that change that is occurring now, Child, all of your choices will have stunning impact. From the simple choices of food and drink to the thoughts you choose and the friends you keep. It is hard to believe that this can be true, but remember all is entangled with All There Is. The I Am is a very powerful tool. Use it now. Think carefully about who and what to be. Then use it to direct your path with wisdom. For using the 'I Am' assertion is very powerful in this new energy. It would be wasted to use on mundane desires such as beauty and wealth. It reaches far and can cover those wants best in the context of the larger, more critical needs of the planet today. I am Love, I am Hope, I am Charity, I am Compassion are all vibrations that will assist Gaia in the creation of peace on Earth. Hold your light amidst those who have not seen it. For your hope, your joy will inspire those whose hearts have been emptied of love. It is difficult to regain the vibration of early youth when most are trusting and fair and generous with their love. Be like little children again, as I have encouraged in different form. Be soft, kind, open and non-judgmental and see how rapidly your life will become joyful again. Be in peace and know you are loved beyond measure. Share it. It is done.

7

Glorious Life

You are seeing and feeling through the eyes of Source today. All is good in Creation and the units meld together to yield a most amazing and spectacular system of life. Be in this space as long as you can for it alone, raises the vibration of the human conversation with Gaia. She feels your conscious awareness and appreciation. That "tunes" the harmonics of your home planet. That tone reaches beyond Earth and reverberates through the Universe, allowing other consciousnesses to partake in the beauty, richness and love in the moment. They collectively thank you for many have no opportunity to exist in human form. But the glorious life experience can be shared by simply being in, and appreciating the moment through the eyes and "heart" of Source. This is the Day we have all made. Let us rejoice and give thanks. Bless this, it is perfect in the now. Go knowing you are loved beyond measure. Share it. And so it is done.

8

Create with Love

And now you know. You create with the force of love. Love drives creation. You can ONLY create with the very powerful force of love. That is the key. As Abraham teaches, learning to hold greater time in the vibrations that are love or appreciation or close to those vibrations allows one to mold the clay of creation. Without love, there is no 'electricity' to power the devices. Without love, there is no energy to shape the physical. Love forms are endless and one need only adapt forms to one's own preferences. All love is power. How one chooses to use it determines the well-being of the Universe. You are all loved beyond measure. Share it. Share it through your creation.

Love Powers Creation

9

Speak Only Kindnesses

Words carry power. Words of love and compassion should be always first to cross your lips. Humor, next and of course, information. Criticism, sarcasm and cruelty are no longer a part of the world order in the new energy. Much as the saying of the tail wagging the dog, words can empower you or castrate you, depending on the intent. Therefore, intend always to say kind words, loving words, and words without sting. As this becomes habit, your thinking will purify and follow suit. And no, my Child, there is no middle ground. Words of hatred, foul gossip, criticism, judgement set up their own energy and fuel the darker side of your world. Banish that energy by shedding holy light all about you with the power of words. Think about this if you have any level of disbelief. Think of what words have done in your own life. They have brought moments of ecstasy, states of well-being, joy and sharing. They have united you in purpose and bathed you in the warmth of love. They have also triggered devastation in your life and others'. Think about this and vow to me once again, that you will choose your words with care and speak only kindnesses. As the Masters go, so you have to go. It is done. Know that you are loved beyond measure. Share it.

10

Choose Trust

Free choice. You, humankind, have the blessing and challenge of free choice every minute of every day. The deer in the forest do not for they have only one path, "one choice" to seek food, to stop and rest, to explore. Learn from the wild ones to do and to be as predisposed in all things. It is infinitely simpler, much less stressful for most, and the path to true peace in the body and mind. All choice can be made with the assistance of Spirit. Invite him/her into your life. Trust your concerns to Spirit and watch and learn the peace of it. For there is nothing too great, no problem too large, no fight too embittered that there is not a solution from and with Spirit. Be open. Be kind. That is all. And trust that a solution will work itself out in perfect time. Do not concern yourself with survival worries for they will be taken care of with ease, like the sustenance of the birds around you. Focus on the ideal - the way you want to be and how you want the world to be. See only that. Honor only that and the rest, my Dear Ones, will fall away. And yes, prayer works and helps. Not in the manner of supplication, but in the style of affirmations of the ideal. Visualize, act as if peace and love are already permeating the consciousness of all. And it will be. You are loved beyond measure. Know it. Share it.

You Have Help

11

You Have Help

One night past the full moon is a bridge day. It is a beginning of a new Earth energy of the Fall planting season. Why is that important? It is important because the seeds that are planted this day, this month will mature to be strong, supple, resilient so as to survive the cold of the winter harvest. So, like this, is the set of seeds that you plant today. The strength and resilience of the outcomes will stagger you. For the greater plan, the greater good depends on those of you who can know the way of peace, love and abundance. And, who can show the way of peace, love and abundance. In all things. Under all circumstances. Stand tall and strong like the winter wheat - yet supple to bend in the wind and resilient enough to bounce back from under the crush of snow. For you are Divine entities pretending to be human for awhile. As the winter harvest is gathered, so too will all souls eventually join together and know their truth. The power of the Merkabah is there for all to see. Open your eyes to the spirit within. Learn in quiet silence. Know that the voice within is there to guide you to your highest good. Call upon me for you do have help. Call upon your own Inner Self, your Highest Self to provide assistance in all you do. If you will join with me each day, we will create each day anew. And together we can easily realize a constellation of entities who will live in peace and love and the wonder of Spirit. As we are all emanations from the Creative Source, we all have the similar longings for joy during physical life. Know Dear Ones, it is not long in coming. For some, they will know it in this lifetime. For others they will know it with new physical bodies and greater sensitivities of the senses. All told, Child, it is truly a blessing to be in the physical on Earth at this time. Each and every one of you is part of the plan for the highest good. Each one of you has contributed to the awakening consciousness of your planet. Each of you will take great joy in the knowledge that you were here to steward the earth to ascension. And so it is that you are loved beyond measure.

12

Pure Thought

Speak only kindnesses. Speech is the utterance of thought and both have power in the now. The best way to control that which comes in vibrational manifestation via sound waves is to learn to control thought. This implies and means all thought. Conscious and unconscious. You ask how that can be, for if we are not conscious of something, how can we control it? The answer is simple. As you focus on kind words, kind gestures, you become more proficient at it, holding the kind vibration close to you. You will attract kindnesses, also. Over time, the unconscious fears, insecurities, hatreds and resentments will mellow as nothing will occur to strengthen those "unconscious" drivers. This is the basis of the directive to be pure in thought, word and deed. For they are connected and even in ways you do not understand. Practice the vibration of kindness, kind words, first to yourself. All day, every day. As you continue, it will generalize to those with whom you have contact. It is a beginning … to learn how to speak only kindnesses. You are loved beyond measure. Share it.

13

Release Fear

It is I, Jeshua. We are connected, hand to hand, heart to heart, for I mirror the Christ in you, who is all powerful as a Creator. Your intuition and ability to be clear is optimal in early morning when the cobwebs of the mind are weak. But your resistance is lowest late at night and after wine or other alcoholic beverages. It would be of benefit to your intentions if you could optimize these cycles. No, it does not call for drinking alcohol in the morning, but by using each respective time for its own optimized purpose. There is a method to this that you may use, or not, depending on what you choose. In the evenings, as you slow and loose resistance, write. Write from your heart and trust that the intention will come across when there is little to impede the message. Learn how to look into your heart and know what should be shared to uplift and that which is best left unsaid. Now take the material and turn it inside out so the beauty, the comfort, the hope and the peace shine through the words. Be not afraid for your words and mine will be welcome. I am here to assist, love you, and pave the way. It is difficult beyond belief for you to trust. I, your Christ, ask you to consider releasing your fear and trusting in me, and Creative Source, like you have trusted no other. Yes, as you ask I will present you with signs, evidence, proof that this is safe, comforting and an expression of love, the love that God Source showers upon all. All are called to this Table - similar to the Mass, to partake of the sharing of the essence of love of Christ as your rightful inheritance. Know and more importantly "Feel" how much you are loved. It is immeasurable by your standards. Bask in the Light of our love and know your way forward is clear and beautiful. Peace. And, so it is.

14

Embrace Yourself

Today, Dear Ones, is a bridge day for you. For today you must make your choice about how to proceed. Your path is calling and I am waiting. And, yes, it is the path of least resistance for it has been pre-paved for you.

This time is a time of change. You have changed Dear Ones, and all about you has changed. There are fewer close to you now. You have no real encumbrances. Only those you create and imagine hold you back. I encourage you, Dear Ones, to let go of your old life and everything that goes with it. Embrace your new radiant self - with self love, and acknowledge your powerful essence - the power to heal, to know and to manifest all that your new heart desires. Yes, the butterfly is a symbol of your transformation. Welcome into my arms. I will lead you, take care of you and love you like none of this Earth. Like none - other. Know me. Acknowledge I AM within you even as the host is imbibed. I am you.

Continue saying only kindnesses to yourself. Your malaise is the result of a disbelief in your power and perfection. As you practice, your disbelief will transform to knowing and you will walk only in joy and peace with me. Know you are loved beyond all measure. Go and live your love. The new energy will make it easier than before.

Transform

15

Channel Love

The crucifixion was not complete. It is true that I suffered in the physical, but it was for no one's "sins." For my Children are all innocent, and there was no logic in my dying for sins. What good does that do? None. For what would be the benefit? Nothing. I was persecuted, much as many of you were persecuted, for questioning the laws of both the Land and the Jews and for disseminating and modeling a message of love and peace. Fear was the basis of my trial - tribulations. And it is true that those of a compassionate heart brought me down and cared for me until I was able to live out the remainder of my years with the Magdaline and our children. Yes, there is direct lineage upon this Earth but my DNA has become so diluted it is unrecognizable. This is nonetheless a blessing for humanity, for every continent, every race, holds a piece of me. Through this multi-dimensional activation of the DNA of my children's children, the Earth's people will come closer to achieving peace than at any other time in your history. Be joyful and know that there is a greater plan in the works than you, my Child, can imagine. In physical you share my DNA. I can provide greater efficiency if you ask. All my children can experience the powers of God-knowing, communion and healing. It is insured in the Galactic laws. Few have known that they are granted that for which they ask in purity and with the intention for the Highest Good. Others' manifestations are also given but there is greater resistance so the manifestation is slower in your time.

It has been through the intentional misrepresentations of my teachings that my message to each and every one of you was distorted. Take this knowledge, sit with it and begin to understand your power as an extension of Source. You can do all I have done, and more - Oh, so much more. Walk in the blessings that you are granted, for you are loved beyond measure and few of you realize the power of that bestowal of love. Use it. Shape the new world with the power of love. Channel it into your projects, your mornings, your casual conversations and into the self-talking in your head that you do so often. Be grateful that love is such a malleable force. Share it.

16

Ride the Wave

Dear Ones, It is I, Jeshua who sits with you. My love can be felt with your freeing your mind and riding the wave of feelings in your heart. Yes, it is true that a symbol, a picture, an icon can assist. Be not afraid to testify to the powerful feelings as they grow deeper and more frequent with your practice. As we are one with All That Is, and your reality is so transitory. I am here with you and all who ask that I join them. For as the new Earth energy assumes its role more and more of my children will be in need of counsel and greater understanding of the ascension/uplifting of humankind. This will be a long and gentle process. But all who are in the physical will experience some degree of change. Change in thought, motivation, words and the relationship to your sun and Gaia. I wish to comfort those who need comfort and encourage those who step easily and willingly into the Light. As the COM led you to know, there is little in your physical world that is not illusion. The remnants of holy love are still a powerful force in your/ our world. Be patient. Be kind and be satisfied with knowing who you are … a beautiful and kind and magnificent Being. In this knowledge, you can do no less than act accordingly, as I have told you. Know who you are as an extension of my Essence and know how deeply loved you and all my children are. For truly you are loved beyond measure. Feel it, know it, be comforted and at peace in it. For this is All That Is.

17

Wake to Love

Have you looked for it? Have you felt it? Slept with it? Have you taken it to your breast? Thrown your arms around it? Have you fed it? Nurtured it? Asked for it? To be a tangible part of your experience? Here is the love within you. Wake to it each day and nurture it in your heart, with intention, as I nourish and nurture you. For it is within you that the love arises, not from without. The Creative essence dwells in your perfect bodies and responds to your crafting as a Co-creator. Feel the love within and know that you have the power to mold love into any form you choose. But it must be your choice. So know this, Dear Ones, it is your opportunity to be deliberate in your creation. I invite you to please use this power. Wisely, if that be your choice. In service of the Highest Good, the Plan, if that be your will, in service of humanity and Gaia as you are called. Know that it is the Divine love that dwells inside of you, Children, that saves the world. Be as a Master and look within to shape and nurture all. For in the stream of creation all is one and each of you are woven through the whole. Be at peace with your feelings, for they evolve with your choices. You are loved beyond measure, for how does one measure the love in this Universe? Know this and go in true peace.

18

Peaceful Earth

This day truly is a new beginning. The numbers are 9-11. It will be experienced throughout the world as a day of peace - whetting the appetites of all nations in the desire for more. More peace, more stability, more unity. For now, on this day, the world unites in their memory and sorrow and compassion for all those who joyfully met their end to deliver such a great gift. The beauty of the global longing for peace is at hand. It will be realized gradually, across all nations during your lifetime. For you, while unaware, have impacted this moment in time. As the pebble thrown into a lake spreads out expansive rings to connect with all water of the lake, so too does your presence and demeanor bring comfort and love to the Universe. You will begin to see more of this as this next chapter of your world's spiritual journey unfolds. Know, Dear Ones, that you have help at your call - all the creative forces are waiting and willing to co-create with you this new, benign, peaceful Earth, always the focus of Creator's consciousness of you. All is well in this new beginning. Be at peace for you are loved beyond measure.

You Are More Brilliant Than The Sun

19

Recognize Your Divinity

Again, Dear Ones, the day is represented as an ending. The closing of the chapters of hatred and war is at hand. It is true it is not yet Universal, but today the balance of earth Energy, that which is measured by Gaia has shifted into the new energy of love and peace, tolerance and understanding, benevolence and compassion. From our vantage Earth will most probably never return to barbaric existence. I ask you, all of you, to play active roles in speeding along the spiritual recovery of this beautiful planet and her children. As known well by previous groups of earlier civilizations, the best you can offer to the Universe each day is your gradually increasing pure vibration. As you learn to live in appreciation of each moment - as you learn how to translate love into your desires, as you recognize the Divinity within each person you meet, the Earth will hear your intent and will co-create with you a higher vibrational calling. It is no surprise that My Children are learning this so quickly - for there are a great many teachers now and a growing number of listeners - who are begging for the knowledge of how to feel better - how to connect with the God Source within. I beseech you, Grand Children, to merely ask - ask for the love of Christ to dwell in your hearts. Ask for all benevolent outcomes to result from your pure intentions. Ask for that, for yourself, which is in the Highest Good. For as you ask you will receive. Only those who abandon their beliefs that they are not worthy will realize that manifestation for the Highest Good.

Know Dear Ones - and this will provide both great food for thought for some and disgruntled resistance for others, that there is no such thing as sin - the way it has been defined in your religions. There is only closer and farther connection to the God-Source, the Creative Energy. Those who live in lower vibrational energies, are more Earth-bound and only have glimpses of the true reality of Source. They, however are not completely separated from Creator at any time. They too, in time, will come closer and may drift away. However one chooses is part of the Divine plan for expansion of consciousness. It is with truth and elation that my heart now knows the hearts of most of my children, and greater and grander expression of love throughout the planet. Be still, be at peace in the knowing you are grandeur and magnificence and the expression of Love beyond measure. Hold that vibration of love. All is well.

20

Pure Intention

I am like a Good Shepherd as I do know and love and embrace my children, like sheep. But my embrace comes from within. From within each of you flows my love, my connection, my embrace. Know that you are an extension of Deity - just the same as I once was. You too have the capacity of Mastery in your DNA - but most importantly in your minds. For intention and will are the most powerful tools one can implement in service of the Highest Good for humankind. Pure intention for good is an often-used phrase but has little meaning for most people. Pure intention is the conscious decision to focus and route mental and physical energy toward achieving a specific outcome. While the outcome need not be specifically visualized, the powering by love to allow it to be for the Highest Good is essential. Essential for the release to the Universe - that will take that intention and move Earth and sky to achieve it in the power of love for all. All good. All beings. All eternity. Only Spirit beyond the veil knows what this Highest Good is. Trust knowing that it is without fail and that your benefit, my children is, of course, a part of the Highest Good. Think on this and offer your mindful thoughts and prayers and thanks in the spirit of relinquishing all but your will to choose - to choose good. You need not know how it all comes about. You need only to wish it, see it, feel it and know it is coming to you. Your lives can be peaceful, joyful, warm and abundant. Wish it, see it, feel it and know it is at hand. You are loved beyond measure. Use the channel of love to move mountains, create rainbows and to envision a peaceful Earth of great comfort. Peace be with you.

21

You Are Connected

My heart is your heart, Dear Ones, those of you who have accepted me, my love, my light. It pulses with life in synchrony with the pulse of the Universe. You, Child, are connected to all that is with every fiber of your Being. You have senses that see, touch and experience the Universe on a much grander scale than you can imagine. So, look around you now. See the beauty, touch the grandeur and realize there is multi-fold more beyond that you see that is part of the fabric of All That Is. The fibers run through you and connect you to every other Being. Not room for even one to fall away without changing the integrity of the whole cloth. Be cognizant of your role in this life and all that transpires beyond the veil. You are greatly loved beyond measure. Know you have a critically important reason to be here, now, and always. And it is done.

22

Lovelight of Spirit

I am here. Within you. In your heart, your breath, your cells. For I am life itself as you are. Only choose that you will know me and you will feel my presence. But more than that, you will begin to honor those around you, for they, too, are enveloped in the lovelight of Spirit, with me. They, too, are one with All That Is. They too seek for soul satisfaction on this plane. So carry the message of my teachings forward so that all my children will know that they are the Divine in a transformed state. But only for this brief time. For through the passageways each must travel into and out of material existence as they decide. Most of the eternal beings on this planet have focussed some piece of their consciousness in the physical time after time, to experience, share and expand All That Is. For without life and the choices made in the physical, all creation would stagnate and just Be. Unchanging, unfocussed, uninvolved. Although love would continue to permeate All That Is, there would be no manner of expressing love. It would just Be.

Understand, Dear Ones, that life, your life, is more precious than you now know. More precious to all Creation than you can see. As you move through your day, be aware of the essence of love being expressed all around you. In the sweetness of the air, the beauty of the water, the grandeur of the trees, the company of the birds. Enjoy this life Sweet Children, for this can be the heaven of your dreams. Certainly, you have the choices in front of you. You can be love, joy, kindness and compassion to All. Or you can choose to be selective in your expressions of the love that you are. Know, there is a difference. A difference you can experience and it will bring you comfort and joy. You are loved beyond measure and We want you to Feel It. All is done.

Beauty Surrounds You

23

Seek Within

Know your own mind. Know what it is that you want. Ensure that your wants align with your ideals, ideals that you are free to choose. Be wary of looking for solace in the things of this world. While you may have all that which you ask for, very little in the physical world will satisfy. There is a longing in each of you, my Children, that is born with you. A longing for the warm lovelight of home. A longing to be in unity with All That Is. Memories buried deep beyond the veil call to you now more than ever. These longings will guide you to seek and find the satisfaction of experiencing the full measure of your own Divinity. Seek within. Know this with your mind, your soul and your heart. Then, and only then, will you feel satisfied as the thirst within is quenched not by that which is physical but by the free-flowing love of Spirit that engulfs you eternally. Child, you can do no wrong. Know that you are here for a joyful expansion of God. All else falls away through time by transmutation. Yes, the violet flame is a functional concept, for it can be activated in one's reality to burn through all malcreations of humanity, leaving only residue. Residue that can be used again as building energies for good. So go, my loved ones, and fear not that you will make mistakes or commit sins. As you align with your true self, your eternal Beingness, you will be loved and guided in all things. Take great comfort in knowing you are ALL protected now in this new energy if you have purity of intention in your heart. Be quiet now and feel the love around you, for you are loved beyond measure. Use it. Use it only for good. It is all.

24

Practice Love

Teach today by your example. Yes, practice kindness and kind words to yourself and to others. There is no need to be haughty or self-righteous in the new energy of cooperation. State your intent and know that All That Is will maneuver to meet your intent.

It is not complicated. However, in this world of free will, you Dear Children, often do not think of or know your intentions. You walk on the Earth and meet circumstance after circumstance with surprise, annoyance and sometimes, distress. If only you would come to know it can be easier, for there is a state of mind that does not allow this to happen. Practice being open. Practice being kind. Practice the feeling of love even when there is no one around you. Practice the feelings of appreciation and compassion. For in the dwelling in these feelings you will walk into kinder and more gentle experiences in every day. Each minute is another opportunity, each heart beat another chance to dwell in inner peace, love and heart. The lovelight that is you must start to shine first in you, for you. Only then, as you become well-practiced can your light shine so that others can see. So teach through your example. Know that those around you can sense your feelings and they often react to them. Give them only love and kindness to react to and surely Dear Ones, you will come to build a new world. A new world where all humanity at some time will feel and know that they are truly loved beyond measure and they can dwell in that love as they choose. Know it in your heart. Be it.

25

Blending Consciousness

My Dear Ones, this is a time of rejoicing. Each soul now on Earth and each beyond your vision has achieved a spiritual milestone that surpasses attempts throughout your history. As the consciousness of humanity merges with Gaia there is a blending of consciousnesses.

26

Expect Ease and Grace

Today is a change point. When numbers add to 3 there is catalytic activity that will spur on change. Thank change [that] comes soon in the shape of the winds that blow in the new energy. Many of my children will begin to know my peace, for they are being called to move toward who they are in these bodies and their true reason for being a part of this Master Plan at this point in time. As you meet others and go about your day to day activities, let all know that they should celebrate and feel great satisfaction in knowing they played a part in the resurrection of the Earth. It has only been through each man and woman's free choices to be loving, kind, generous, compassionate and peaceful, that the consciousness of Gaia was able to absorb this magnificence and move away from the Armageddon of past prophesies. Now, Dear Ones, there is only kindness in your futures. The Earth and the stars with all of Creation will look upon you with sweet benevolence. Pray with joy, expect ease and grace to follow you. Know that your many lives have been of utmost value in bringing humanity to this day, the edge of a new time in space. Your future lives on this

planet will emerge into a more peaceful and blessed evolution. You are loved beyond measure. Bask in it.

Note: In reality, there is no space or time. In humanity's reality there is.

Hand of God

27

You Touch All

All is well with your planet in the now. However, fear and malice and worry of those who inhabit the Earth can hold her back. The vibration of mankind, due to the emotional tone each individual emits, sets the tone first for Gaia and that translates into the tone of the Galaxy. The vibrations mingle, and bounce and in each way they interact, all is changed, all is continuously transformed. This can be the consequence of pure and benevolent thoughts and deeds or the result of fear, insecurity, hatred, and warring. Choose peace Dear Ones, but it is peace that must be your choice. No one else's. And in the grand Master Plan the works and words of each of you will ring out through the Universe to touch All. Know it is the power of love that elevates each consciousness higher and higher. If you can capture and hold the Feeling of Love in your Being the consciousness of all that is around you is elevated. Know it is the Feeling of Love, of compassion, of appreciation that has the power to bring about the Highest Good for All That Is. It is not in using the word 'love' without feeling the pure emotion that is effective. It is not in mimicking the deeds of lovers that consciousness will be uplifted. It is only through the deeply felt and pure emotion, passion for your life, that each of you can more easily connect with us that you call God. It is now, in this new energy, that it becomes possible for each child to more easily select that path for him or herself. For it is in the intention that each of you draws power. And there is much assistance as you need and as you ask. There are immeasurable benevolent energies at your back waiting to push you forward into ascension consciousness as you give the word. These angelic energies intermingle with your pure intention to bring about that which you and only you determine. You must learn to be more comfortable with choice. For choice is your only real responsibility in this life of yours on Earth. And, as you choose, so follows the world for each of your power is truly felt in far distant realms. I ask you Children to choose wisely for in those choices lay the future of humankind. Believe there will be energy fields to push forward toward anything that you want but realize with depth of knowledge it is your, and only your responsibility, to cleanly and clearly choose what you want, who you choose to Be and how you intend things to work out. If you allow others to choose for you, you will be waylaid. It is from the depth of your Spiritual Being that your true knowledge of who you are resides. That is the inner knowledge that, if left untampered with, will guide you to your true purpose of living in and through the Light. Know it is the embodiment of the eternal and immeasurable love that powers your Universe. Know, Child that each of you is part of that flow and that nothing you can say or do can change the truth that you are loved beyond measure. But everything you choose to feel, say and do determines whether the Love that originates with Creator, Creative Source continues to flow to you, through you in an unobstructed way.

28

New Transformative Energy

There are important dates that arrive on your calendar. Many through the second half of the year. Do not fear anything, for it is important that the Earth vibration is not hampered by such vibrations as fear or hate or arrogance and aggressiveness. This is a quiet time spiritually when you will all be assimilating to different extents the transformative energy that is being thrust upon you. This is a great gift and one for which you have held great intention to achieve for many lifetimes. All souls on Earth will feel the benevolent nature of this. All souls will gradually transform, some to a greater extent, depending on what their baseline spiritual vibration is now. Many will seem unchanged but do not judge, for this is unwise. As you will eventually be more able to recognize the divinity within, Children, your eyes still cannot see. Each of you contains the divine Creative Source and continues to live eternally, sometimes in physical and sometimes in non-physical. There will be a lunar eclipse some call a blood moon. This day marks the beginning of an era where there will be no blood shed on Earth for reasons of war, aggression or greed. For at the same time, the new energy is assisting in funneling away negative energies, so they no longer hold power. But Children, this causes an energy imbalance with now far too much light to balance with the dark. In order to keep the light- one, each one as well as the whole of humanity shall need to accelerate their own vibration at least a notch above that of the past. This will allow a rebalancing of the Earth's field to now hold a very different balance of light and less light rather than dark. And, you will know this to be true as you see acceleration of the gentle removal of dark power and the replacement with leaders of logic, of kindness, of understanding and compassion. Your Pope is a trigger to allow light into hearts and places where it has not been before. He is truly a Lightworker, and his light touches so many. Go then, my Children, and bring light and hope to those in need. They may not see as clearly now as you, but they will also move from less light to more light in their appropriate time. It has been said before, you must go through this process. ... but each soul can make its choice of when. This is the advancement of the Consciousness of Creative Source. It does not and cannot stand still. Forever changing, forever expanding and forever improving the brilliance of the Light. There is no end to the light that feeds the immeasurable love that Source sends to you.

Forever Changing

29

Focus Your Thoughts

As the child knows no fear when he or she is held closely by a parent, I want my children to know no fear. As this day of great importance wanes, all will see only benevolence. It is the greater plan. None of the destructive scenarios can take place now that the required .5 of 1% of the faithful have focussed their energies on elevated consciousness. I call to all who hear this to relinquish your focus on the Doom and Gloom scenarios that the dark energy has employed to control you. Look only for the light - the light in all things and move toward that light. For where there is joy there will be more joy. Where there is love there will be more and where there is peace, it will become more peaceful. But in the same way, dark emotions of hate and greed and resentment will attract even more dramatic situations to foster their growth. I invite you, Dear Ones, to separate yourselves from all negative thoughts and feelings that do not serve you and the Higher Good. Look at yourselves as you hope, think, and act and evaluate closely if those are in alignment. You have great help for the asking. Ask each day, each morning, and you will soon discover that those days will yield only good and lead you closer to joy. Ask and it is given to you though you may take awhile to see it. Know that all of the powerful forces in your realm will stand forever. You are greatly loved beyond measure. This is an important day, an important time to become who you choose to BE in this Universe. There is no end to love and eternity. Your earth is a crucial part of the evolution of consciousness. It serves no one, nowhere, for there to be the devastation of the planet. Each soul group has challenges, many born of the weather and geological phenomenon. But those will lead to growth. Trust. It will be so.

30

Choose Carefully

Today is a sort of portal. It is a day that a window opens for those who want to see beyond that they choose to see daily. It is not the only day for there will be a number of such opportunities in the coming 2 years that will have the same power. Much of the power of these portals comes from from stellar alignment and the course of Earth through fields of energy (radiation). Fear not, for there is only kindness and joy lying beyond these portals. If you choose - that is - if your level of intention is pure then you may access information, visions, insight and grander communication on these days than on others. Use this day wisely, for the manifestations of your choices will come swiftly and have wide impact. Choose carefully your thoughts today. Focus only on glory, joy, utility and peace, if that would be what you choose your life to look like. Share emotional messages of love if you would choose to receive them. Praise all in your path today if you should want praise. And live every moment deliberately. For it is in our intentions that humanity can set the destination toward which we travel. May all the blessings that come as a result of this portal be shared with all humanity. Be joy. Be love. Offer comfort. Be an ambassador of peace and you will know only that in your life. May you know also that you are loved beyond measure by all the hosts and energies of the Cosmos. Source energy is a protective and benevolent energy. Have belief in that so you may go about your business with confidence and share hope to inspire those who want to believe. It is your task, Dear Ones, to shine the Light of Christ on any path that is darkness; Christ the Life Source.

31

I Can Assist

If your heart is heavy, clear it and then we will talk. Remember I am within you and can assist with the tools you have been given. Breathing meditation is meant for exactly this. Go in peace, Child, for you have much to consider. You are loved beyond measure. Take comfort in the aid you receive.

Know the Sun Shines at Night

32

Seek Me

I am here with you now even as the light, the breath, the stars are with you at all times. Though you may not see the light during the night, you know it is still there, cuddling your planet's under-belly as you sleep. Even though you cannot see your breath on most days, you feel it moving in and out and through you. Even though, when it is daylight you cannot see the moon and stars, you know they are there. And you can feel in the wind and the tides their influence in your lives each day. Know this now. I am always with you, and in you and surround you. You cannot see me but you can see the riptides, the wave, the calm that are my influences in your lives. Know me as I know you. Seek only the good in your self, for that IS ME. Seek only the good in your friends for that IS ME. See only the good that comes from dire circumstantial happenings and know these are the consequences of my influence in your lives. You cannot know in this realm how much you are loved for it is beyond measure. You can, however, trust that because I am always with you there is peace, there is joy, there is kindness and love within you. All you must do is open your eyes and seek it.

33

Do No Harm

Act in ways that are harmonious with your brother's and sister's way of life. Act in ways that are harmonious with nature. When decisions are presented to you, ask first, will this decision hurt or impede the life or freedom of another? If so, choose otherwise. When faced with an action in your life, ask first will this decision harm life, hurt the Earth or fester into a larger problem in the future. If so, choose otherwise. As it goes, many of my children believe they have little choice about so many aspects of their lives. And, as you believe, it will be. But if you believe there are, or can be, better choices, more options, less negative burdens on the earth - seek such change. For as more and more conscious souls ask for "a better way" more and more minds are prepared to hear, see, discover and share optimal solutions. This principle can apply not only to legal decisions, parenting, your workplace but also to life choices about where to live, how to heat your homes, what food you will nourish your body with and how you will create and share pure water. Be in this mind as you go about each day. For as you sow your seeds in the now dictates the abundance you will reap in the future. It cannot be clearer … do no harm. And regardless of your choices, you are known, understood and loved beyond measure.

34

Blend Into Unity

I know you. Yes, like the Good Shepherd, but in many more ways. I know your Light signature, your bands of vibration, the very thoughts that emanate from your mind and the tone of your heart. It is I who am part of you. And you blend into the Unity that is the I AM. For we are all together a Unit in the vast Creation. Though you have no memory now of that belonging, have no fear of death so that you may live fully in the now. Your souls know the greatness of who you really are and please believe or know your grandeur. My heart sings when you turn to me, when you invite me into you so that you acknowledge your Life Source. For it is in the flowing waters of the energy of life that you will find me and the whole of mankind. View your brothers and sisters not as evil or malicious for they all believe they are doing good in their own ways and for their own reasons. Good may have many faces not all of which are tidy and clean or obvious to you. Trust my word that all of the billions of children of the Life Source have the same spark of Lovelight in them. Namaste means the Light recognizes the Light. I invite you, Children, to see no one in your life as evil, as malicious or as deliberately cruel. View them as learning students of the Light. Soothe them, for know they are doing their best. And, most importantly, know they are on their path much as each/you are on yours. Be patient, be tolerant, be Loving for each of you is loved beyond measure. Ask, only ask Dear Ones, to allow yourself to feel and experience the Love of God and, with your pure intent, you will experience the comfort of the Greatest Love Energy in your own Life.

35

Share Your Delights

You need none other than the faith in the true Christ. For there are those among you who would have you believe that there are other ways to cross the veil of dimensionality without first having love in your heart. Faith my Child. For the knowledge that the Christ is your Life Source, your sustenance and your companion in your physical bodies and your Spiritual bodies is, or shall be, sufficient to bring you joy, peace, well-being and comfort. You need not magic. You need not healing Light Ships nor Beings from other galaxies to bring you to peace and healing. You need only daily trust in the gentle ways of the Christ as manifest on Earth in the Master Jesus. You need only faith to bring the Lovelight of the Christ into your soul space. You need none other. Feel this as truth and you, my Children, will have only peace, contentment and, perhaps most calming in the sea of corporality, no questions. Go as you must into the world of your today remembering you go with your companion. Speak with me, share your delights as if I were a partner by your side. Feel my attention, my love as I deliver beautiful flowers to your smiling face. Be joyful that I am with you and that you are connected to the Spiritual. Go now into your day in the knowing that I am with you, part of you, in you and always expressing my/Our love of you to you. For you are loved beyond measure. Take comfort in that knowledge and know that no harm can come to you when you walk under my Wings of Love. Peace. Remember peace.

Energy Surrounds You

36

Learn Through Living

Listening alone to my words does little good for, as you know from Others "words don't teach". For my words must be felt. Must be experienced, must be lived to be of value to you. As they are lived, you too, can move toward Mastery. Learn from my example, not my words. My example is all about you. I am the gentle lover, I am the fond parent, I am the wise teacher. Look about you. I am in many who you already know. See the kindness. See the effects of kindness, expression of caring, of love. And then behave in the same manner. You will soon learn from experience. And learning through living is a much richer, deeper and committed path to My heart. We are all in this new energy together. Yes, I am back with other Masters. Not in the physical the way you knew me before but in the physical energies that are all around you. That move to you and through you. This is why so many of you who ask Me are receiving channellings. And of great importance is that they are all consistent as the receivers can be free of bias. The message is the same. You are loved beyond measure. Know it. Feel it. Take refuge and comfort in Our Love. Be then as you really are, and live it in all you feel, think and do.

37

Yourself First

Listen. Each of you, Listen. Listen to your body's cries for soothing. For, I am in you and must also listen to your body's irregular heartbeats, cries of discomfort and pain, labored breathing and shallow breath and the noisy struggles of your belly and intestines. These noises that can be heard, by me, by you and by others are signs and signals from your innate body of wisdom. They represent a calling to you … to eat no more, to stop drinking that carbonated soda, to feed yourself more natural produce and, to treat your bodies with love, respect and gentleness. Do not appease a craving without knowing what the temporary comfort will lead you to. Do not use in excess food, or drink, or relaxation of the body. Instead ask your cells, your heart, your gut, what would and would not be beneficial. As you focus your attention on your query, you will hear a response. So listen. Listen to the quiet voice in your gut, your heart, your mind, that tells you quickly what the body prefers. Yes, muscle testing is also a route to the same information. I urge you My Children, to take measures to feel good in your bodies. To be enlivened and full of vigor and strength. For unless you feel the perfection of your bodies as they were meant to be, you will have great difficulty in focussing on that which is meritorious. It is hard to be kind when you are in pain; hard to feed others when your nutrition is deficient; hard to think clearly, meditate or pray when you have aberrant chemical reactions throughout your body and brain. It is with love beyond measure that I gift you with these words. Look after yourself first, and only then can you be of loving, giving service to another. As in another's words, "you are of no use to anyone if you are sick". And, yes, you can heal yourselves. I will give you more on this another time. Be satisfied in your physical bodies for they were made to share with the Divine.

38

You Always Have Impact

There are infinite ways that each of you, my Children, are connected to the Universe. For you, your energy, your souls are infinite in time, in space and in potential. Even as you go about your daily business, your vibration, your affect pours out of you shedding light on that which is in your environment. You always have impact, exert influence and it is by your choice whether those influences will be positive or negative. How do we look at or define positive as separate from negative? Go into your hearts for you already know the answer. Positive influence increases love, appreciation, harmony and peace. Negative brings on strife, discomfort, worry, anxiety and hatred/warring. The influence is clear in the consequences. For if the thought feels dark it can only draw to it and result in dark or negative consequences. If a thought or act feels right, joyful, good or benevolent, no matter what your eyes tell you, that thought or act can only draw to itself positive consequences. You may not see this. You may feel ineffective. But know Dear Ones, the rules of nature, of the Universe, are unbreakable. As you practice to choose only positive thoughts and act out positive deeds you will soon find how little you have been able to see (how closed your eyes were). As you practice kindness and learn of it's power in your Universe your eyes will widen and you will rejoice. For the Master Plan unfolds, with or without your assistance. But know that your ease, your joy, your participation is at stake here. So choose wisely Dear Ones. As you choose, rely on your Higher Self to guide you, your knowing and feeling, to lead you, and the knowledge that you can do no wrong for you are loved beyond measure in infinite time and space. Go in peace, for whenever, your time will come.

39

Compassion for Self

Find in your heart the roots of compassion for yourself first. Feel the trauma and tragedy of your own life and then marvel at where you are - your heart is now - through my intervention and with my Love. Contemplate that today. Recall the depths of sorrow, the fear, the resentment, the injustices that you have experienced - some with a pure heart; others with a closing heart. Know, today, your times of famine, emotional upheaval are done. In my Lovelight, in this new energy your life will become a fairy's tale of love, laughter and life. It is done. And, only now after you fit together the puzzle pieces of your own experience and view it with the perspective of compassion for yourself can you bring hope, truth, love and compassion to others. For each of you has by this time endured a great deal. Know that many still are choosing to endure more. See these extensions of your own soul with only love. Give them the hope that you now know is real. Give them a hand, when they need it, food and shelter when they ask. I am your hand, your nourishment; and find shelter in my arms. Dear Ones, there is much to be hopeful for. Lean on those around you who have already discovered their peace, their joy. For they are the ones who can show you the many choices you have to attain the same place of joy, peace and love. It requires little of you but a purity of thought and a willingness to see the world in a new light … literally THIS new light. For the wonders of who you are, your power, your connectedness to Source are being realized slowly but by many now and tomorrow. Rely on each other for love. Rely on each other to deliver peace. For it is in the eternal love of Spirit that you are all known and know that all seek the same. You are loved beyond measure and it is through compassion for yourself that you will eventually learn to recognize that which deserves compassion in others. Be peaceful, at peace and be hopeful for all that is benevolent waits for you to choose it. I leave you with great love, great hope for your journey into today.

40

New Energy Within

As all days, I am with you, in you, and enliven you. It is not so difficult to understand if you know that there are forces and energies unseen in your world. The energy in the oxygen flows into and through you unseen and yet you know it delivers life force. The flow of gravity moves through you and around you and allows your bodies to operate as they should. The forces that glue your cells together, indeed the very molecules that hold you as you, are unseen, but you never question their existence. There are conglomerate unseen energies about you, in you, each influencing your body, your thoughts, your environment. I have seen the benefits of you learning to live with microwaves, UV light, telecommunications signals and radio-waves, all unseen energies. Now I ask you Dear Ones, become open to yet another. The Spiritual energy that runs through you is becoming more 'felt' by all those who are sensitive to it. This is an unprecedented opportunity to learn to work in this new energy field with the Spiritual Energy of the 'I Am.' As you have seen great benefits from working with electric and magnetic power, you will be astounded at the magnificence of that which you may accomplish within the new energy fields. Know that

I am a Master and dwell within you. I am a Master who will teach you if you seek this wisdom. Know I am the Master of Life and the Source and can show you how to harness the powerful energy that I AM in You for <u>all</u> you seek.

Light Meets Earth

41

Manifest What You Choose

In the beginning there was the "word". This word is synonymous with intention for Creative Source-intended expansion of conscious mind. The Light was manifestation of intent and malleable through the power of great love and intention. The light became physical - the Earth, Sun, Moon, Stars, are all differing densities of light energy. As is humankind. The light condensed into human form is quite dense indeed - say compared to your sun. But in this new energy of the Universe, the earth absorbs more light and other energies. So human bodies absorb light energies that may or may not be seen by some of you. As those energies are absorbed the body becomes less dense, more pliable, of greater power to flex and change. The combination now of these new-found energies with love and intention can powerfully manifest that which you choose. If it is perfect health, tell your body with love and pure intention that is what you choose. If it is peace and calm in your environment, look with love and pure intention and see only peace and calm. If it is beauty and harmony that you want to surround you, use the energies at hand, mold them with love and pure intention and create that which you will. For the creation story is not history. It is ongoing reality. It is the example of how Creative Source continues to change, expand, yes, propel newness through All That Is. Be not afraid to use your newfound powers of Creation. But choose well, choose wisely so that the humanity that is in all of you benefits. If you come to me - Christ the Life Source, before committing to a creation path and ask for assistance, I will guide you - with all of the love the Universe presents without measure. I will guide your steps, and bring you to a less dense state of Being.

42

You Are Provided For

Give away that which does not serve you. I mean get rid of everything you have little or no use for. This means people in your life, services that you rarely need, and the things that clutter your space. Then, and only then, can you focus on that which is important and that DOES serve you! This is your time in meditation or prayer, time preparing and consuming nutritious food and drink and time interacting with those precious souls about you. For much of the time you now occupy with trivia related to things, people, places. Trivial pursuits that bear nothing, no fruit. That give you little in return. It is fine to keep those items that bring you pleasure when you look upon them or use them. It is fine to keep those friends who uplift you and for whom you serve, and it is fine to continue those practices that yield you more time to do as you choose. For, I wish you to see, Dear Children, that your time is indeed best spent in an awareness of that which is beautiful and bountiful around you, in a state of appreciation for all you encounter and an affect that reflects goodwill and joy. For this is the State of Being which encourages the higher vibrational fields around you to attract more that serves your higher consciousness. Be in the moment and you will never be without all that you need, For it is gathered here, in my hands.

Even that which you have no knowledge of is prepared to meet and satisfy you. You need not know the mechanics of this but believe that it is truth. For once you accept that, you can release your fears, change from concern about survival to trust and knowing you will be provided for. And so much of that which is prepared for you is in the spiritual and superconscious zones that bring you much greater benefits than anything in the physical. Go, My Children and greet your day with feelings of awe, and love, with a sense of adventure and a childlike appreciation of all that comes to you. Yes, these are deliberate choices, for you still, after knowing this, have the choice and the power to disregard. In that case you will continue with your petty concerns, your clock of events and the polishing of your pretty things. But in no case will any of that activity bring you joy - joy like the joy you may have if you do these things in a state of bliss. For this reaches far, sustains itself and the world and raises the vibrational energy of the Earth, of which you are a part. Go now, and make your choices and know full well that in whatever realm you choose, you are loved beyond measure. So do that which is right for you.

43

Choose Peace, Love and Joy

Many of you feel the new energy within and around you. It feels so much more tangible and powerful and up-lifting. Yes, Dear Ones, you can partake in the fruits of this new energy. Easily, with grace and knowing. For the most awe-inspiring moments in your life are about to come. The moments when you realize that it is within you … .the power, the grace, that which is Divine. As you choose in pure thought you will begin to feel a greater connection, a greater clarity in your tether to your Higher Self - your soul, if you like. It is in that connectedness, which is much easier in this new energy, that you can communicate with Spirit more directly, feel the benevolence and love of Creative Source and manifest your life as you envision it. Be aware young Ones, that the benefits of envisioning a world of peace and joy and kindness and your role in bringing that about far outweigh the benefits of envisioning a life of wealth, beauty or fame. For those have already been expressed at one time or another in your string of eternal incarnations. The wisdom those lifetimes have brought you is available in your Akashic Records. They are there to aid you in understanding the magnitude, power and magnificence of who you are. As you become more aware and more comfortable with that image, you will be able to move in this world much like the

Masters before you. For each of you has within the makings of the Masters. If you choose to envision your life modeled after any of those, you will move in the direction of peace and joy. Not only for you, personally, but for the planet. Your willingness to choose an expression of life in a higher vibration of peace and love and joy brings a higher vibration to Gaia and elevates all. Know that you are loved beyond measure. Share that knowing. Share that love which is unending. In it, be at peace.

44

God Needs You

Is there a way to initiate communication between what is called 'God' and man/humankind? And the answer is YES. The beginning of a connection has to do with openness to being out of control. Not the out of control that comes with drugs or alcohol or the resistance associated with ambition. What is an essential characteristic is the resolve to TRUST the almighty. To know deep in your heart there is no better way - the almighty 'has your back' and you do not need to worry about anything. For all is as you have determined through your choice. What you do not realize, Dear Ones, is that 'God' is here to do you service - to meet your needs, to share your joy. For it is with the experience in the physical that the needs of 'God' are met. It sounds foolish that 'God' has 'needs'. However the driving force of All That Is merits the new knowledge - the expansion of consciousness that each one of you bring in each moment of your existence. Be thankful that you are in physical form now. For this is a time of great joy and celebration - throughout the Universe. We are going together into another realm, another time, another existence in order to perpetuate the sanctity of life. Be at peace for all is as it should be. You play an important role in the manifestation of the Divine on the Earth. Go in joy and peace. Share love and the contentment. For you deserve ALL that is blessed in this realm. You are loved beyond measure and that is the way of the Christ. Go now in peace.

45

Energy Exchange

Take the task of hunting for food - the type of hunting warriors of other ages needed to perform to enable their bodies to be strong, healthy and able. This took much effort and focus and time. In those days, the animals would present themselves to aid and assist humankind. There was no torture - man knew how to kill swiftly. There was no stress for the spirit is all knowing and can vacate the physical before the time of trauma. You have seen this and call it "freezing". Some associate this with fear, though it is not. There was a balance between men and their animal food that was respectful. Man somehow knew that this was their only means of deriving adequate sustenance. And it was the men, primarily, because it was the men who warred, battled and travelled without comforts of a home. They often battled weather, illness, rodents that would prey on them.

Why do I tell you this? What does it matter? I tell this to you because it is important that you know what purpose hunting served, know that animals came freely to assist mankind, and that the energy was truly an exchange. You need to know this in order for you to derive more energy, nutrition, benefit, from your food now. Many of you eat meat and fish that have been alive. And this is fine - an efficient manner of providing your bodies with key nutrients. This is fine, for those animals and fish offer themselves freely to your world. However, one thing has predominantly changed. And that is, that there is no longer an energy exchange - it has become completely one-sided as humans take and give nothing back to these glorious selfless creatures. If this one-sidedness continues, more animals will choose not to release their bodies for food for humans. Many will exit by plague, illness, and other means. So you ask, how can mankind restore the energy balance of old, now at a time when there are few hunters and animals are often "farmed" in conditions that many humans consider cruel? I tell you now be less concerned with their conditions for they know and freely engage in the physical experience. Be more concerned with the energy at their time of death and at the table where their flesh is converted to your energy. As the advise is simple. Say, feel and express greater thanks and appreciation. Do this as you take their lives. Do this as you sit at the table and consume. For it is by your thankfulness that the proper honoring and energy exchange can again become balanced. Soon, in this new energy field you will be able to see more clearly the energy fields of your food and it will become more real to you. Yes, reinstate the old practice of saying "grace" before you eat but not in the rote manner in which families offer only words. Rather, acknowledge that the animal on your table presents itself freely to you for your sustenance. It presents in a manner that preserves and sustains your energy, for you did not need to hunt for it in most instances. Know the honor that this animal deserves and feel the wonder of the true exchange of energy - your conscious appreciation in exchange for the dense energy of flesh. You do not see how these can truly be equal to balance out. Trust in me that they are, for the vibrations of thanks that you offer at the table resonate through the fields of earth and the galaxy and serve to balance and invite more spiritual energies to come to you this way. So I tell you be far less concerned with the free-range chicken and farmed fish and more concerned with your attitude towards them. And you will find as you share your awareness of their role in your life, that the nutritional value of your food will increase. You will eat less, be more satisfied and experience improved health. Even such a simple thanks at breakfast and dinner each day can, if offered in a true spirit of appreciation, do much to improve chronic disease states such as arthritis, Alzheimer's and diabetes. I invite you to try this for 1 week and note whether you feel different. And, later we will address your consumption of plant life, for there is little difference. Go now, find your nourishment and be thankful, for it is an expression of the unmeasurable love that is here for you.

Offer Thanks

46

Synergistic Energy

All the Beings of Earth will soon know there is greater history in your past than you can imagine. Yes, the gods of old were in some ways gods. Yet they were, at a time, very corporeal. Most have now moved onto a higher plateau of existence. It is part of your growing up process to be aware of where humanity is headed in this new energy. I tell you that it matters little whether you and they fly in planes or saucers. It matters greatly that you choose a peaceful existence. As new technologies come to your planet they can bring great wasting or great advances. As with these choices, so goes the consciousness of mankind. I urge, no, invite you to explore with dignity and respect all the choices available for the uses of the new knowledge that is now being uncovered. It is in the intent of those who are close to it, who touch it, that much of the way of the world will go. Be aware, Dear Ones, your intentions synergize with theirs. This is a wonderful time to pray, to bless your leaders and to ask all non-physical love source Beings to work with you to fulfill/satisfy your intentions. For this is the time of the ripening of the fruit that you have toiled so long to bear. Taste the sweetness of the nectar. Enjoy the scent and the texture of peace, of love, of cooperation among all the nations on Earth. For only in joy, not fear, can all mankind walk together, hand in hand, heart to heart, into your brilliant future. Know I will be there with you as these discussions progress. Know that there are legions of non-physical Entities and energies at your calling. Invite them, direct them with your pure intent and watch and behold the miracles that ensue. For all the Entities join as one God in loving mankind beyond your ability to know. So take this fully in the manner in which it is given and press forward in love and Light.

47

Flavors of Thoughts

All the Entities of Our Presence rejoice when you rejoice, love when you love, appreciate when you appreciate. And so it is that your experiences lead to an enrichment of the I Am. Your experiences can be on the joyful end of the continuum or the hateful and fearful end of the continuum. It is your choice that controls whether we are experiencing with you or not. When you choose love, kindness, compassion, understanding, charity, you feel good because We are there in you, with you, about your experiencing the positive vibrational tone. When you choose feelings of fear, envy, animosity, hate, we cannot feel those emotions because they are so far away from our vibrational states. You feel worse with these emotions because We are not with you and you become more distant from "God Source." As I have emphasized, you have the power to choose and control your feelings by disciplining your thoughts. This discipline comes in two flavors. One is rigidly adhering to your beliefs of righteousness, your deserved power over others and your cravings for physical dominance. The other flavor is characterized by a joyful acceptance of what you encounter, a flexibility of mind and a determination to remain joyful and ride the higher vibrational path to wherever it calls and takes you. You each know, Dear Ones, where you dwell. Those of you who taste joy and love and kindness will soon learn to discipline their thoughts, words and deeds to remain in that good-tasting space with us. Those who choose the path of attempting to dominate their world will never succeed as their bitterness contaminates all they touch and experience and moves them farther from peace and joy. Bitterness can be camouflaged by sweetness. Learn now to choose sweetness, kindness and loving thoughts that can help you cover any bitterness that lies within.

These simple practices reflect the consciousnes of the Masters and they are ready and willing to assist you. All you need do is ask for they respond to your call. You are loved beyond measure and All That Is is committed to serve you in great love. Go now, knowing your choices will come to fruition as they express grace and kindness to All.

48

Earth Vibration

All is truly well with your world. There is no Armageddon or End coming to the life on the planet for the love that has moved consciousness to a higher level has removed this threat forever. Fear not for there will soon be a huge shift in the balance of light and dark that there will be few left on Earth who are dark enough to cause such harm. Yes, this will take several generations but what is that but the blink of an eye in all Eternity. The face of the Earth, Mother Gaia, now smiles with hope, love and gratitude to the children she has birthed. The Mother feeds and sustains her children. She provides them the energy to live, to love, to thrive. But each child must decide for him or herself how to direct that energy. What to do with the fuel in their lives as they move farther from the womb. Know your Gaia sees you and feels your connection now even greater than ever before. Mother Gaia is welcoming the new levels of consciousness and assisting in the transformation of humanity. She will continue to work with all to deliver a peaceful, beautiful loving shelter here on Earth. It is for the benefit of all the souls who have chosen to mold this environment over hundreds of decades and for the benefit of the non-physical Entities who experience and expand as a result of your Being in this time and space. All that you think, feel and do is recorded in a sense and contributes to either raise the vibration of Earth or lower it. For as you choose your thoughts, feelings and actions, so goes the world.

Earth's Creation

49

Clean Intentions

Your body is a reflection of your intention and the expression of who you are becoming. It is hard for people to understand that their will plays a great part in determining how they feel and how they look. If a man says "I want to look handsome to this woman" then, if all else is neutral he will appear to her as handsome. If he says instead "I know I am not good looking, I hope she doesn't mind" then the woman will perceive him as not good looking. You see, Children, perception is real. Corporeal presentations are only real when they are perceived. If your intention is to be kind or generous or ambitious in many instances, this will be how you are perceived. So first, think and choose carefully. Each day. With each interaction for this is a powerful tool. It has limits however that you may not always control for the perceiver also has their own intentions. Sometimes these may be neutral but more often the perceiver is already intending to see you as healthy or sick, competent or incompetent, attractive or ugly. So the melding of intentions determines, for each, their own perceptions. In order to move onto a path of easier and more beneficent energies you shall need to be aware of your intentions. It becomes important that they are 'clean' and free of hidden motives. For many of my children interact less in pure love and good peaceful intention but with the motive of controlling, gaining, or using the other. Sit quietly and realize your intentions and then dismiss any that could be perceived negatively. This practice will bring you excellent results, peace of mind and generate goodwill.

50

Greet Your Day

"Tidings of comfort and joy."

51

Soul Energy

The Spirit within you is always connected to your higher God-self - Inner Being - Source Energy. Though you may not be fully connected, you are never disconnected, while you are in the physical or non-physical. Source is always a part of you. Many call it soul or essence or life source or prana. This is the part of you that exists in different forms eternally. It is similar to the experience you have with water. In its liquid form it is dense and heavy and has specific uses in that form in the body. As the molecules of water vibrate at a higher rate / frequency of vibration, the molecules move farther apart and you see the rising into the air of less dense water molecules in water vapor with the help of the energy derived from a hot stove or the sun. As the molecules continue to absorb sun energy, for example, they rise and vibrate very rapidly into forms of clouds. While each piece of cloud appears distinct in the sky to your limited vision, the water vapor in truth is a continuum of molecules vibrating at different rates. The water is always water, regardless of the rate of vibration, whether you can see it or not. It permeates your atmosphere. Soul energy is somewhat similar. It has always been and is always changing. It vibrates on a continuum of levels - sometimes forming distinct entities, sometimes just permeating all that is. This is the best analogy to try to let you know that your soul is not singular. It is a merge of soul material, soul energy, that is continuously re-surfacing its physical inter-relatedness with humanity and changing with humanity's vibrational output - which is the energy that is used to shift soul vibration to make it more or less connected to you. You are never without soul - never disconnected - much like you are never without water in your body, your breath, your air and all around you. The unmeasurable love that is all around you can be directed by your choices to expand your soul's material or to contract it. This is to help you better understand the nature of soul, though it is quite an oversimplification. Know, if nothing else, that you are a single soul in many physical bodies and that your spirit is continually merging with, clustering, distancing itself with and from other soul material. Much can be learned from watching the clouds. Go, knowing you are loved beyond measure and that your soul already knows this and uses love to power its continual expansion.

Ethereal Soul Material

52

Seek Peace and Wellbeing

That which seems unhealthy, evil, filled with hate, usually is. Your ability to discern what serves you from that which does you harm is becoming more refined in this new higher energy vibration. And that is how it should be if it is your will to live to enjoy the sweetness of a long and joyful time on this planet. For as you learn to recognize the triggers that make you feel the opposites of love - that bring you fuel for hatred, vengeance, animosity, cruelty, you will also learn to reject those triggers. The movies that depict torture, the news that documents the occurrence of hate crimes, the soldiers that destroy each other, bring you only negative emotions that do not assist you to live in joy and peace. Recognize that which brings you "down" and learn to discriminate those triggers from that which is uplifting, that brings [you] to joy, appreciation, contentment, and feelings of warmth and love. Know the path to these feelings and seek them often for in that state of being - one of wholeness with Spirit and wellness - you offer to the Universe the highest gift that you can give. It is not just in actions that spiritual grace is manifest for even the 'biggest' action offered with resentment or in discouragement will be negated if it does not lead to a higher vibration in all who are touched by that action. It is far better to "do" nothing than to offer actions that are not pure in their intention. So, Children, seek only the feelings that serve you. Those are the feelings of love, hope, gratitude and joy - that will sustain you and add power to the Universe. Your world, Dear Ones, requires that a new, stronger energy evaporate the energies of your malcreations (in thought, word and deed) and transform them into a healing wash of rain. They can be transmuted, every malcreation of your past and past lives at this time, merely by stating clearly your intent and why. For my Dear Ones, it is only in the seeking that you can be found by Spirit. Seek peace, love, communion with all that you deem good and your vibrational state will soon reflect your pure intent, pure thoughts and choices for action. Know fullwell that you are loved beyond measure, watched with loving eyes, and wrapped in a blanket of warmth and security if you choose to realize it. Believe it so that it may become a way of your "Being". Be all This.

53

Know the Christ Within

Be at peace. At peace within yourself in the knowing that all is well. Your soul moves through changes. It is the natural way of 'evolution' of the soul - as all souls are dynamic interconnected entities. The soul moves about in full knowledge of who you are and what role you play. Your choices direct the merging with other aspects of soul and the dissolution of other aspects in your realm of time and place. In truth, Dear Ones, it is all merged in the Being of God consciousness. It is in the movement of soul that God consciousness expands. Soon, although not in your sense of time, those of us who inhabit the Earth will begin to be able to recognize Creative Source in their own consciousness. This is the state for which it benefits you to strive. This is the state where you know and feel the Creator within. This is the state of allowance and communion with the Christ - the Life Source. This is the reason that you chose to incarnate to merge the 'best' of the physical with the perfection of Source so that All Beings can enjoy the sanctity. Know the Christ within. Converse with your God essence. Use your belief to know you can create that which you choose. Know in full the depth of soul and the unmeasurable love that lies within you for you. As you move through your day, stop and ponder the wonders of the love within. You shall have the choice to do no harm to yourself. You choose wisely. And thus, there is no cause for concern, for all is well and you can exist in a state of peace at all times. Feel the love that accompanies you everywhere. Go in peace.

54

Co-exist With Creator

There is little time to waste. Be in your body fully today and experience the bliss of coexisting with your Creator.

Created by Source

55

Who Promised?

Broken promises need not concern you. Promises should be delivered with discretion. Promises are often stagnant and stagnating which contradicts the dynamic laws of nature. Your state of being is ever-changing, so how can you lock yourself into promises when you do not know who you will be in the future? Promises lead to expectations on the part of others - expectations that are often difficult or impossible to satisfy.

Your promises come in many forms. Perhaps the most insidious are those you make to yourself. The promises to lose weight, not to lose your tempers, to treat your children with kindness always. These are endless promises that create only the useless feeling of guilt when you fail to keep these. Instead, Dear Ones, look only at each moment, as it arrives on your plate. Decide in each moment what serves you best and then choose. Sometimes eating more is an entitlement; loosing your temper an appropriate conveying of emotion; and disciplining your children an important teaching tool. Let loose the promises to self. Realize that all is dynamic and you change with new energy each moment. Do not think that static promises have a lock on your life - for if you do believe that, then you choose to give away your free choice - free will in each, beautiful dynamic moment. Stray not from your intentions for betterment but "go easy" on yourself.

Another set of promises are made to each other. The marriage promise is perhaps the most apparent promise that is not, nor can be always kept. As each person in a relationship changes, so should there [be] opportunities to touch more or different lives. Remaining bound by old promises that no longer serve you allows an institution to control your free will. As in all matters of humanity, the institution of marriage and divorce were put in place to control economics. These institutions no longer serve individuals. A more effective approach that would produce less pain, different expectations and result in more healthy relationships would be temporary joint arrangements. It would also allow for cultures to address the main blights that arise from broken marriage promises. It is the wise one who will understand that promises given will rarely meet expectations. There will be negativity on the part of the other and guilt on the shoulders of the promiser. This serves no one. Be at peace with this knowledge. For in each one's life there is evidence of the truth in these words. Know you are loved beyond measure and however you choose, we love you no less.

56

Teach With Your Heart

All of your days are spent in lavish comfort with little inconvenience. Rarely do you have the chance to encounter someone truly in need. In need of support, love, of someone being there for them. For most in your world look outside to their God and not inward. They do not look and therefore do not see God in their fellows/brothers. There is one who presents so that you can learn to teach. Slowly at first. Then there will follow more opportunities for you to share the wisdom with those who seek. Right now be patient, slow. Open your heart and follow the signs. There will be ample chances to assist and enlarge your brother's hope, trust and knowledge of the Divinity within. Speak kindly, offer kind gestures, do not promise things that are beyond your reality to provide. Say loving words for they lead to expanded love in all directions. Be still. Feel the unmeasurable love that surrounds you and ties you to every other man, woman and child on your planet. Feel this. Know the truth in this.

57

Feel the Connection

We talk of love and the way the body reacts to love. As many know, love produces changes in the chemistry of the brain and body. And love powers even deeper changes in the body that you can neither know of or see. But you <u>can</u> feel those changes. When one receives love there is a healing. A sensation of comfort, kindness, trust. When the mind is in this state you become "more" connected to God. When you are connected, your body knows what is needed for your optimal health and it goes about its business of renewal and healing. When you feel love for another person, place, view, thing, food, the body also becomes more connected to All That Is and energy flows through you to the object of your attention. Therefore, by giving love, you benefit from the connection with God and the object of your attention also benefits. It is much like a 'two for the price of one' sale! You are so loved. Share it.

58

Building Bridges

There is little value in wallowing in depression or self pity. The world has chosen to make these medical issues, and indeed they can be treated as such. Bear in mind these states are ACTIVE choices. Yes, it is a form of response to your world when you feel out of control, not free to make your own choices. Know that is a weak argument to soothe the self in the physical. The reality is that periods of self pity, deep sorrow and depression are times of renewal. They are breaks from the routine of your life system that provide the opportunity to 'reset' your awareness. Your awareness of who you are, what your role is and what you want to be. In themselves, periods of self-pity and depression or sorrow are not bad or negative. View those times as bridges. They are indeed the bridges that you build by choice to move you from one state of Being to another. Therefore, realize you ARE in control as the builder of the bridge. You <u>have</u> exerted your free will to choose to escape your current state. Honor and appreciate that you have fulfilled a great action when you move from self-pity, great sorrow or depression to a more comfortable state of conscious awareness. Know this is a mechanism that can serve you well if taken in small portions. Use your own light to guide your way. Seek the betterment of your state with free choice. Whereas, some allow these states to rule their lives, know that, too, is free choice. Be open to assistance to help you move. There are eternal Beings that, as you call, will come to your aid. Be open. Trust and know all is well. You are loved beyond measure.

Choose to Move Forward

59

Listen For God

My heart is lifted in joy when each of you communes with Spirit. For it is in this communion, both physically, as in the Mass, and spiritually that the new methods of speaking to God are born. God is all knowing and sees and feels your heart's intentions. God Source is beneficent so that all who ask are guided in love.

All those who pray, talk with Spirit and are open to listening will be in the new light of awakening to the word of God. Their words from God. In this new era of disciplines that will connect mankind's ear to the word there will be a new acceptance. Acceptance that no one is more or less worthy to be in direct line of communication. You need no priest, Master Teacher or yogi or channeler to touch the heart of God for you. You Child, are worthy, fully worthy to receive your own words from God Source. The conditions of such communion are straight forward. First, you must invite God/Spirit/Source/Creator into your heart, mind and lives. While many feel they do this, it alone is insufficient. This must be paired with pure, joyful intent. Intention to live and love [in] the manner that is given through the words. Intent is key. Not that all who endeavor will be successful in living and loving in a continuous way, but as more of humanity is able to do this, there will be greater gifts bestowed. The gifts that come to those who commune with me, the Christ, and All That Is, will lead you to a physical and spiritual life that is filled with peace and contentment, love and joy. Be who you Are in your communion with the Spirit of All That Is and your days will reflect the unmeasurable love that is wrapped around you.

60

Moving On

Pain is all in the interpretation. Each of You, my Children, will experience, while in the body, a set of conditions that are not favorable to you. There is the physical pain of aging, the heart's pain of lost loved-ones and the mental pain of verbal and physical abuse. It is not to say that pain is not real to you and of extreme discomfort. It is not to say that pain can be ignored and it will always disappear. But pain is a signal to you. It is a clear and unambiguous signal that some circumstances in your life must change before your body, heart, or mind can release the pain. Many times the connection is evident. When knees or hips are eaten by arthritis, it becomes clear that "moving on" is needed. And often that is enough. When there is discomfort from abuse, again "moving on" to your next love is healing. So view pain not as an inescapable fact of life, but view pain as a message from the combined wisdom of your body, your Higher Self or Soul and the Stream of God consciousness that flows to you. With the faith that there is always something better in your future, you can imagine what that will be and "move on" in that direction. Ask your Spiritual Team to support you in your quest and trust that they will lead you. Go without fear, for you know you are loved beyond measure and no harm can befall the <u>real</u> you, the you that is Spirit, pretending for a time to be human. Go knowing you are well taken care of.

61

Pure Energy

The sun shines brilliantly upon you. It provides warmth when you are cold; light when it clears the dark; nourishment for you, the plants and animals of your earth. As brilliantly as it shines, it does not come close to the brilliance of you. In our spiritual realm all of humanity shines with a brilliance that provides light and soul nourishment to life on other worlds throughout the Universe. Not just your Universe, for we see that your brilliance cuts through dimensions that you do not know of. Together with Mother Earth, Gaia, this world shines in magnificence beyond words. You are a part of this brilliance. You shine like your great star the sun. You think this is metaphorical, but it is not. You are light. You are pure energy. You derive from the Creative Source, God. And God envelopes all of you in the beauty and power of love. I have seen you shine. I know what is possible. I know that you can bring your brilliance unto the Earth as you do just by Being. My love is always with you, powering your brilliance; sending it where it needs to go to dispel the dark. Oh, Child of God, of Mine, Be only who you know you are, a brilliant extension of the Divine. Share your essence, let others see themselves reflected in your light. For as I said, John 8:12 I am the Light of the world, So too, are You. Be at peace within yourself and in knowing you are loved beyond measure.

62

Love Grows

Be at peace. All ways and always. For there is nothing in this world that can harm you - the real you. Remember you are Spirit, powerful Spirit, housed for a brief time in physical bodies. There is nothing in this world of the physical to fear. Nothing you have not seen or experienced before in other brief periods of your previous lives. As others who choose to dispense fear and hatred come together with those of you who carry only Light, their darkness will be dispelled. They work now to bring upon themselves their final death throes. And while their physical bodies die, their spirits return to us to be blessed for their willingness to play such a harsh role for the benefit of humanity. There is no greater love than to give of one's life for his brother. And, that, my Dear Ones, is what is going on in your world today. For the violence, the hatred, the public cries for death to the bodies of others serve to assist all types of humans to realize, with clear definition, what they no longer will tolerate in their lives. As this moves forth, in this world you will see for the first time on this earth, a coalescence of minds and wills from all countries, from religious groups including those that have spawned this black seed. The minds and wills of the vast majority of humanity now choose, in full awareness, a better way to live on this planet. There is compassion in the hearts of

All and that nurtures the Earth in a way that will lead to the next advances of humanity. Your consciousness will now move to a level of vibration that will allow many of you who choose to reach into the realms where you may commune with Spirit/God/ Creative Source in a deliberate and direct manner. You need only express your intent and desire and you will be pulled close to the bosom of All that Is. There you will begin the journey of feeling the unmeasurable love that exists for you and you will begin to realize it grows continuously. So then you will gladly share it with the others of your planet as they move in the same direction. It is only with love that the Earth has been created. It is only with free choice that humanity has come to sustain Mother Gaia. And, so knowing All is as it should be, go in peace. Today, and all days.

There Are No Wrong Turns

63

There Are No Mistakes

There is a "knowing". It resides deep inside each one of you, My Children. The knowledge that you carry within gives you the power to make decisions of your own about everything that faces you on a day-by-day basis. Yes, you will always have free choice. You may choose to heed your knowing about what is aligned with the path you have chosen, or to set it aside for now. You shall continue to have innumerable opportunities to re-align yourself with your Inner Being or Higher Self or Soul Purpose - whatever you choose to call this. And, My Child, you know this also. So there is no such thing as falling off the path; you may choose to go faster or slower, take pause or detour, but you cannot - cannot fall from your chosen path.

Rest at ease then, with the decisions of your life; the big ones and small ones are really quite similar. You cannot make a "wrong" choice - only a choice that will delay or accelerate you on your chosen path. Stop riding the waves of guilt for past choices. Stop dwelling upon consequences of current dilemma. Even as your choices define you here in the physical, your choices direct you in the non-physical realms. Again, I say get in touch with your Inner knowing to keep you aligned from day to day, year to year. When in doubt, sit quietly with your heart. When you need assistance, call upon Us, your Angels, and Guides, the Christ and Source, for ALL are here to love you, respond to your wants, and, as you ask and choose, make it easier for you to express and feel your Inner knowing. There are no mistakes - only round about ways to get where you are going. All paths lead to the same. Enjoy your ride, enjoy the pace, be uplifted; for in the knowing that you are taken care of, you are finally free to Be all that you choose to Be on this path called Life.

64

Eternal Unmeasurable Stream of Light

There are no words to describe the stream of energy perfection that is 'God' or 'love' as you call it. For humans do not typically know all the aspects of love simultaneously. They experience something they call "falling in love". This is different for them from 'true love' or a 'Mother's love' or the love of a pet. Only rarely are the energy and feelings melded together so that one can come closer to experiencing the well-being and benevolence of Creative Source. All That Is is merely differing expressions of the energy of love. It is not the love that you know, but eternally present, magnificently powerful and unending. As you choose, you may partake in this love that is Creator. You may momentarily commune with Source energy. The more practiced you become, the closer you move to All That Is. There is no difference between giving love, as you know it, and receiving love, for it is an eternal unmeasurable stream - of Light, of kindness, of well-being, of comfort.

As one looks upon the Star of Bethlehem, there will be more conscious awareness of the closeness of God within you. Speak of peace, speak of comfort, speak of joy, for that is what is brought to you now, and will be evident in your skies. Know that there is Divinity within. Recognize and greet that Divinity in others and watch the glory of a New World unfold as you become more enlightened with this new energy. Know there are some of you who will set the stage for this new era of peace. It is in the words of Christ that you are invited to love your brother - all brothers - so that the unfolding of a grander, more peaceful world will emerge. Thank each individual for being a part of this time of transition. Go now in peace. Be aware that it is of your own choosing and feel the comfort and joy of Being a part of the unmeasurable stream of energy that you call "love", but will never fully know in the physical. That is all.

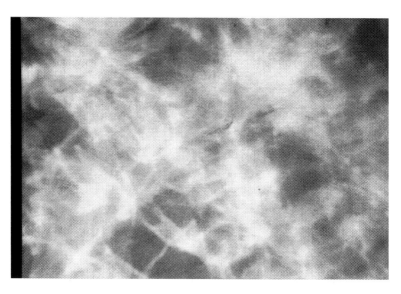

Unmeasurable Stream of Love

END Volume 1

Please look for the publication of Volume 2

Printed in the United States
By Bookmasters